WOMAN
AND
POLITICAL
POWER

BY

LUKE OWEN PIKE, M. A.

FELLOW OF THE ANTHROPOLOGICAL
SOCIETY OF LONDON

1

ISBN-13:
978-1727079227

ISBN-10:
1727079221

IT is not improbable that the present remarkable phase in woman's history may have made its appearance, partly at least, through reaction against the very common opinion that the male is the superior sex. This idea, offensive as it is to all feminine sentiment, receives its best illustration in the old fable, according to which, various parts of the body, each being necessary to the rest, put in a claim, each, to superiority. The truth is that in the sexes, as in the members, there is neither superiority nor inferiority; but it does not therefore follow, as has been hastily assumed, that there is equality. No two things can be pronounced equal or unequal, superior or inferior, unless there is some common standard by which they can be measured. The color *blue* is not equal nor inferior, nor superior to the color *yellow*; and the *green*, which is produced by the mixture of the two, owes no more to one than to the other. In the same way, humanity is perpetuated by the coexistence of male and female; and, if the functions of either one sex or other were radically changed or perverted, humanity itself would cease to exist.

The most vital point in my present argument
is that woman must be regarded as woman,
not as a nondescript animal, with a greater
or less capacity for assimilation to man. The
question, regarded from a scientific point of
view, is not how far the female intellect can
be trained to imitate the male; but what it
may be shown to be from observation, or
inferred to be from correlations of physical
structure. The argument, from observation,
which would be considered sufficient by
most men of science, is controverted on the
ground that human laws have been stronger
than the laws of Nature. It is said that man
has oppressed woman by his superior
muscular power, and has impeded the
natural development of her intellect. If this
be true, and if mere strength of body can
thus get the better of mind, it is certainly
strange that horses and elephants have not
become the masters of men; and hardly less
strange that the stalwart Negro should long
have been the slave of the more intellectual,
but not more muscular, white man. But, as it
is useless to prove the relations which have
existed, to those who preach of relations
which ought to exist, between the two sexes,
it becomes necessary to investigate the
matter from the point of view of physical
structure and its correlated functions.

Among other and better known features distinguishing the female sex from the male, are the smallness of the brain case, the width of the pelvis, and the tendency to deposit adipose tissue, rather than muscular fibre. To the rule, of course, there are exceptions; there are masculine women just as there are effeminate men, and those exceptions I propose to consider before concluding, but they ought not to affect the broad general treatment of the subject. To these and other differences of structure, correspond numerous differences of function. Both the capacity and the desire for muscular exertion are less in the female than in the male; the strength of the system develops itself in another direction. So also the desire, if not the capacity, for the prolonged study of abstruse subjects, is less in the female than in the male; and mental activity pursues another course. It does not follow that, because a man can lift a greater weight on the average than a woman, he is therefore her superior, any more than that he is her inferior because she can bear children and he cannot. Nor is woman man's inferior because she has never devised a system of philosophy, any more than she is his superior because he lacks all her wealth of maternal tenderness, and some of her ready powers of expression.

Much has been said of the difference of
weight in the male and female brain; and it
has been argued that the female intellect
must, for that reason, be necessarily inferior
to the male. But apart, from the difficulty of
finding a common measure for the two,
there is great uncertainty concerning the
relation of mental activity to the contents of
the skull. The average stature of women is
less than that of men; and therefore the
absolute difference of weight cannot be a
fact of any value, unless the various mental
functions are localized. He would be a very
bold man who ventured to pronounce that
the brain has no influence over the muscles
of voluntary motion, or even over those
which are beyond the control of volition.
And when inferior stature is found in
combination with less development of the
muscular system, who can say how far these
conditions may be the correlates of some
condition of the brain? It may be, and
probably is, true that the brain is intimately
connected with intellectual and emotional
manifestations; but it is probably no less true
that the brain is connected with all
manifestations of volition; and, until we
have determined the relative position and the
quantity of cerebral matter necessary for
combined muscular movements, we have no
means of determining the quantity or the

position of that which is necessary for thought and feeling. I am aware that many attempts to localize the various functions have already been made; but the mere fact, that the various inquirers and experimenters have arrived at various and contradictory conclusions, is in itself enough to prove that the Contents of the skull have not yet been correctly mapped.

Women of all nations are, I believe, generally considered to possess not only more emotional characters, but greater powers of observation than men. If this be true, it follows, I think, that their senses must be more strongly developed than those of the male sex, and that their memories must be equally if not more retentive. It matters little that the objects which they observe are not the objects observed by men. It is as great an effort for the eyes and mind to see and remember all the colors and all the forms in a room full of human beings, as to define the position of the earth's strata, and assign every fossil to its place. But women, on the average, prefer millinery to geology, and men, on the average, applaud the preference. The matters with which attention is occupied must, to a great extent, depend upon the bodily capabilities of each individual. The man who has lost his limbs cannot scale mountains, and the blind man cannot paint; but the energies of either may flow in a direction suitable to his circumstances, and each may distinguish himself in some field of thought.

And so, although woman may be more at home in the drawing-room or the nursery, than in the field of battle or the seventh heaven of metaphysics, her walk in life may exhibit qualities as high, and energies as well directed, as those of the chemist, the engineer, the philologist, or even the philosopher. Nothing can be more ungenerous than to flout her with her domestic cares, or to depreciate her efforts to please. If her form is more susceptible of adornment than man's, it is but natural that she should be more anxious to adorn it. If it is a privilege of her organization that she can become a mother, the wish to deprive her of it is not consistent with the teachings of science, with manliness of character, or with common-sense. If her maternity forces upon her the consideration of minute details which are unobserved by men, or have no interest for them, the tendencies of her mind are not a fit subject for detraction, unless that detraction be intended, as it commonly is, for maternity itself.

The *elements* of the female mind (to regard the mind alone, for a moment) are probably, as the champions of women's rights assert, identical with those of the male; and the inference which some persons would draw is that the *mind itself* ought not to be different. No one would seriously deny that woman possesses emotions, will, senses, and intellect; or that man's mind is susceptible of precisely the same division. It does not, however, require even a knowledge of chemistry to discover that combinations of the same elements, in different proportions, will produce compounds of different qualities. But chemistry, perhaps, illustrates the subject better than any other science. Not only may the same elements, mingled in different quantities, produce substances of different properties; but the same elements, even in the same proportions, may, under different circumstances, yield dissimilar products. Not only do the ethers differ from the alcohols, and each alcohol and each ether from its namesake, though all are compounded of carbon, hydrogen, and oxygen, in different proportions; but alanine and sarcosine—which are both compounded of carbon, hydrogen, nitrogen, and oxygen, in exactly the same proportions—have properties entirely different from each other. If, therefore, it could be shown that the male and female minds are, in the language of chemistry, isomeric, it would not follow, according to any natural law, that they should be identical in character; still less if they merely possess the same elements without being isomeric. And it would surely be not more unscientific to preach the conversion of all ether into alcohol, and all sarcosine into alanine, than to insist that the feminine mind should undertake all the functions of the male.

While the senses, and the faculty of retaining impressions, are as strong in women as in men, and perhaps stronger, it will hardly be denied that in all ages and in all climates women are and have been more prone to the display of emotion than of pure reason. Rachel weeping for her children, Sappho burning with desire, Iphigenia grieving, not to die, but to die unwedded, Aspasia brilliant with wit and cruel in hate, the girl who, as Horace says, lied gloriously to save her lover, the woman prodigal of her ointment upon the Saviour's head, Cleopatra, too proud to live when she could not captivate her conqueror, are immortal types of what is good and what may be bad in feminine nature. It is not out of such qualities that statesmanship can be developed or science advanced; but science

11

and statesmanship are not the only good things in the world, and the world may enjoy enough of them without calling in the assistance of women. If man's highest prerogative is to think, woman's noblest function is to love; and this assertion is not a metaphysical dogma, nor even a generalization from the history of mankind, but is an inference from the relative position of the sexes throughout the whole of that class of animals to which mankind belongs. The maternal instinct, as it is commonly called, is shared by the females of all the mammalia, from the tigress to the gorilla, and is not, as might be inferred from certain teachings, the sad consequence of iniquitous legislation.

The skull of the female gorilla differs from the skull of the male, just as the skull of the woman differs from the skull of the man. And this difference has not been caused by centuries of oppression; it merely gives evidence of the healthy operation of that natural law by which structure corresponds more or less to function. In some respects the skull of the female gorilla is more human in its form than that of the male; and so, also, in some respects the skull of the woman exhibits, in a more striking manner, the attributes of humanity than that of the man. Nor are these skull differences restricted to a few species; they extend throughout almost the whole of the vertebrate family; they are accompanied by differences of muscular development, which are no less constant; and the whole of these physical differences are correlated with a psychical difference which is indisputable the greater pugnacity of the male as compared with the female. Considered, then, apart from individual peculiarities, the diversities of male and female capacities may be seen to have arisen from the widespread action of natural laws, and are not to be annihilated by a merely human decree. It is not the fault of the male human being that he possesses more, than the female, of that combativeness which is necessary, not only in political life, but even in the ordinary struggles for existence. It is his privilege to protect, and hers to be protected.

It may be suspected that the advocates of a sexual revolution have been unfortunate in their experience of the sex opposed to their own. There is no doubt that, century after century, women have shown a preference for men possessing the qualities which seemed to them distinctively masculine; and that men have wished their wives to possess the virtues which are considered distinctively feminine. In other words, the intellect of either sex has found pleasure in association with something dissimilar to itself, not because one is better or worse than the other, but simply because the two are different. There is no more reason for the assertion that a woman's brain is an undeveloped man's which requires cultivation, than for the assertion that a man's pelvis is an undeveloped woman's which requires to be expanded, or that some of his muscles should be converted into fat. To him it is not, as a rule, given to express himself so rapidly as a woman; to her it is not, as a rule, given to think so deeply as a man. But she often sees what is lost to him during a fit of abstraction; and he is often indebted to her for the materials upon which his reflection may work. Genius, it has often been said, is of both sexes at once; and the saying well indicates the true relation of the male and female intellects. Each has powers and beauties of its own; each may profit by contact with the other, and it is not until some resemblance to a combination of the two has been effected that men recognize that highest mental development to which they give the name of genius.

There are few subjects interesting to man in
which clever women do not sometimes also
take an interest; and from this fact it has
been hastily inferred that women might,
with profit, devote the same attention as men
to any and every branch of study. Such an
inference leaves out of sight the fact that
women rarely look at any subject from the
same point of view as men; their opinions
often have the value which is to be found in
the observations of an intelligent spectator
when persons, whose whole attention is
absorbed in any pursuit, fail to perceive
what most concerns them. The best critic is
not always a good author or composer; and
excellent suggestions are frequently made
by those who are not fitted by Nature to
carry their own ideas into operation. This is
especially the case with women, who, if they
were to devote their whole energies to
science or to politics, would do violence to
their physical organization. The prolonged
effort which is necessary in order to work
out any great scheme, to make any great
discovery, to colligate any vast mass of
materials by a great generalization, is a
heavier strain on the vital powers than any
merely physical exertion. It is, like military
service, inconsistent with that bodily
constitution which is adapted to maternity,
and all that maternity implies; nor does it

15

seem possible that by any process of selection, either natural or human, this difficulty can be overcome. The change in woman's nature must (if effected at all) be effected either in one generation or more; if in one, humanity must immediately cease to exist; if in more, humanity would only be extinguished by degrees; but the diversion of woman's vital powers, from the course which they take by nature, is neither more nor less than the abolition of motherhood. And this, either wholly or in part, either directly or indirectly, is what some earnest men are preaching in the name of sexual equality.

The modern attempts to deprive woman of her womanliness belong to the metaphysical school of thought, as much as any dogma of a medieval schoolman. They start from the assumption that living women either conform, or should be forced to conform, to some *a priori* definition of woman, evolved from the inner consciousness of a human being. They ignore all the ascertained facts of anatomy and physiology. They are directed not toward the perfection of womanhood in all its functions, but toward the transformation of woman into something different. They suggest not the study of natural laws, nor the observation of facts in

Nature, but the worthlessness of all facts, and all laws, in comparison with a dictum issued from the study. It is not wonderful that ignorant enthusiasts should have placed woman in a false position through their inability to comprehend their own religion, but it is perhaps the strangest feature of the nineteenth century that thousands of persons advocate a still more unnatural revolution of the sexes in blind obedience to a purely metaphysical proposition.

The stages into which Auguste Comte divided the progress of human thought are admirably illustrated by modern attempts to alter the position of woman. Seventeen hundred years ago she was a stumbling block in the way of the religious enthusiasts; to the metaphysicians of today she is no more than an abstraction. The early fathers of the Christian Church regarded her physically as a temptation to sin; some modern philanthropists regard her intellectually as the equal of man. It is possible that there may be truth in both opinions, but it is certain that the whole truth is not to be found in either. The religious doctrine is intelligible enough at first sight, but the metaphysical doctrine takes us back to the middle ages, to the conflict between the realists and the nominalists, to the verbal quibbling in which great minds, for want of better occupation, frequently expended all their energies. The woman for whom a vote is demanded is not, when carefully inspected, a woman of flesh and blood, but an abstract or archetypal idea for which the realists of the nineteenth century claim a positive existence.

The process by which such ideas were arrived at in former times, and by which, in all probability, they are arrived at now, is of the following character: Men and women possess certain attributes, or a certain attribute, in common, and to this attribute, or to these attributes collectively, may be given the name of humanity. All points of difference are by the very nature of the process disregarded, or drawn off, or in technical language *abstracted*; or rather the point of resemblance is *abstracted* from the point of difference. Now, when humanity and similar abstract terms had been thus invented by men who perceived their value as a species of mental shorthand, they were invested with a substantial existence by Plato and many of his medieval followers. The "humanity" which is reached by this mental operation is, of course, divested of sex along with all other differences. If the human beings who are actually born into the world could in reality, *or* even in imagination, be made to conform to this sexless archetype, there could be no objection to voters on the score of sex. Thus much may be safely admitted; but it would then be in the power of any human being to coin such a word as "mammality," or "animality," or to make use of the old word "entity," to assert the existence of a substance corresponding to each word, and so to destroy not only the distinction between man and brute, but between organic and inorganic matter. In short, the very same argument which would introduce woman to man's occupations on the ground of her humanity, would introduce whales on the ground of their mammality, or stocks and stones on the ground of their entity.

I trust that I shall not be considered guilty of any disrespect in reducing some well known arguments of some justly influential thinkers *ad absurdum*. I no more mean to show disrespect by my treatment of the subject, than to deny the sincere philanthropy of many who advocate woman's rights, when I say that it savors not a little of priestcraft. Just as the metaphysical stage of thought bears a great resemblance to the religious, so the attempt to carry a philosophical doctrine into execution is by no means unlike the attempt to impose a creed. Every ideal form of government which has hitherto been conceived has had innumerable elements in common with the Church of the middle ages. From the time of Plato to our own, philosophers have always presented themselves upon the domestic hearth to dictate the relations between husband and wife; all who are acquainted with the early books of penance will remember that the priest took upon himself the same office, even to the minutest details. In all the mediæval works which touch upon science it will be found that the final authority upon every controverted point is not the evidence which may be discovered, but the doctrine of the Church; so neither Plato nor Malthus, nor the followers of either, appeal fairly to physiological facts or laws, but would repress the very instincts of human nature wherever they are opposed to the philosophical idea.

The apostles of all religious and all metaphysical doctrines have commonly been not only energetic but thoroughly honest men. They would direct all thought and all action into the groove worn by their own minds, not from an innate love of tyranny, but from an enthusiasm which cannot admit the possibility that persons of a different opinion may be in the right. In the apostle there is always much to admire, but it happens only too often that his priestly successor inherits his faults without his virtues. The present may be called the apostolic age of the doctrine of equal humanity; and many followers will be won through respect for the character of the apostles, rather than from conviction after sober consideration. But, to the student who desires something positive in science, and who would use that science for the benefit of mankind, there is sad discouragement in the spectacle of a new intellectual crusade for an idea. To this there are only two possible issues—on the one hand, complete failure; on the other hand, government by a metaphysical priesthood which will not even spare sex in its efforts to crush out all individual preeminence.

It may, perhaps, be thought that the Anthropologist who endeavors to assign woman her true position according to the laws of Nature is practically not less tyrannical toward her than the reformer who would have her modelled according to rules of his own. There are, however, two most important distinctions to be borne in mind: In the first place, the man of science knows from observation and experience that when

21

structure is healthily developed, and function of every kind unimpeded, there results the nearest approach to happiness of which any individual is capable. But the Utopian of the a *priori* school gives no pledge for happiness except a general proposition, or a series of general propositions, well enough suited to the days of Plato, but wholly without value in the days of Darwin. In the second place, the propounders of new schemes make no provision for exceptional cases, but would reduce all mankind to one dead level, while variation is admitted, and the efforts of remarkable individuals are watched with interest by the observers of Nature. The latter, conscious that they are not yet masters of the universe, would allow fair play to all alike, in the hope of learning something new; the former, tacitly assuming that the apex of knowledge is reached, would issue edicts, from their metaphysical Olympus, for the reconstruction of humanity.

There cannot be a doubt that human beings exist who, though not of the male sex, have more masculine intellects than many men, and others whose muscular development and power of enduring fatigue are far superior to those of many a conscript. Had conquerors possessed Utopian minds, they would long ago have declared the fitness of women for military service, for which they are adapted just as well as for political life. But it is only in such a work as the "Republic of Plato" that we find a plea for the application of the same physical training to both sexes. In that treatise[1] an objector is made to suggest that the spectators would begin to laugh if men and women were seen struggling together in the same arena. The philosopher, whose ideal republic would have possessed an hermaphroditic army, could not see the point of the joke, and expressed a profound contempt for the sneers of the unphilosophic. It is, however, worthy of remark that, although he would gladly have seen women converted into wrestlers, boxers, and soldiers, and even thought of giving them a share in the government of the state, he declared them to be in all things weaker than man. The idea of absolute equality is of quite modern growth, and has probably been suggested by the undeniable success of the female intellect in many fields of literature.

To write ingenious novels, and even successful dramas, to paint from Nature, to interpret the works of the greatest musical composers, to act with taste and discrimination—all these, and a thousand

23

similar accomplishments, each requiring an effort of intellect, are now within the range of women who are no more exceptional than the front rank of men in every generation. Such distinctions may be attained by women who lose none of the charms of womanhood; and even a knowledge of the latest discoveries in science is in no way incompatible with any of the feminine graces. But a little consideration will lead to the conclusion that all this mental activity is but the evidence of human progress in general, and that its root, as well as its most perfect development, is to be found in the domestic life. Long before the invention of printing, mothers amused their children with nursery-tales, lulled them to sleep with songs, and imparted to them the rudiments of such knowledge as the world possessed; maidens and wives could act well enough to deceive husbands or attract lovers in the days of Homer or even of the patriarchs. And many of those beautiful poetical stories which constitute the mythology of all imperfectly civilized nations bear the stamp of woman's imagination, and have often been narrated to excite or to soothe the terrors of the young.

Women, however, with intellects truly masculine, are, and have always been, even more rare than women with a masculine development of muscles. There are few, if any, distinctively masculine pursuits in which any women have ever succeeded; there is no great law of Nature, no great mechanical invention, no great legal code, nor even any great metaphysical system, of which any woman can say, "Of this the world owes the knowledge to me." A reason for this fact is to be discovered not in the inferior quality of the feminine mind, but in the character of the objects to which woman's physical organization naturally directs her attention. The practice of medicine, which is now becoming recognized as a feminine occupation in America, suggests at once that instinct for nursing, which every one admits to be the special gift of woman, and which is, in fact, a correlate of her power to become a mother. In short, if there be any truth in science, the intellect of woman not only has, but must have, a certain relation to her structure; and, if it could be shown that there exists no difference between the male and female minds, there would be an end of anthropology. But the directions in which clever women have developed their mental activity afford the best possible illustrations of the scientific view of woman's position, and show how the long-inherited instinct matures itself according to the truly feminine type. All the different lines, when traced back, converge through the nurse upon the mother.

It should not, however, be forgotten that there may be individual peculiarities of structure, caused by circumstances either antecedent or subsequent to birth, that the constitution of society may impede the natural development of function, and that there may be a number of women in every age whose case demands special consideration. Though the births of males are slightly in excess of the births of females, the females in the prime of life exceed the males in number, and it follows, therefore, that, even could every male afford to marry, there would still be some women husbandless. The difficulty which here meets us is only one among many of those which appear irremediable not only to statesmen, but to men of science; it is no more probable that the body social will ever be so constituted as to secure the happiness of every individual, than that the human frame will cease to be subject to disease. There is, indeed, no doubt that the science of health and the science of politics are closely allied, and that each must be imperfect without the other. The end of both is the extinction of mental and bodily pain, but that end seems to be unattainable. Anatomists and physiologists know only too well that, had freedom from disorder been the object with which our organs are constructed, the means would have been lamentably ill adapted to the end, that every malady is easily induced, and with difficulty checked, and that the greater part of mankind start in the career of life with some inherited weakness. It is true that much has been done toward the mitigation of epidemic diseases, and it is possible that something may be done toward the alleviation of social grievances; but the success which has been achieved in one case affords a very instructive lesson toward the mode of proceeding in the other. Epidemics have been deprived of their worst sting, not by any political theories, nor by a statement of human rights, nor by a definition of man or woman, nor by a refusal to consider our physical organization, nor by any attempt to alter it, but by a careful study of the facts of Nature, and by placing humanity, such as it is, in a more favorable condition toward the outer world, such as it is.

How the woman who cannot marry may be most favorably placed is a problem which can hardly be solved in general terms, and which must be answered according to the exigencies of each particular case. But it may be safely asserted that the gift of votes to the whole female sex would not in any way improve the condition of old maids; wherever keenness of observation and a retentive memory are of service, there is a good prospect of success for a cultivated female intellect In proportion as the instincts of sex are suppressed, the range of acquisition may be widened. Woman naturally loves to teach the young, and, when she is without husband, home, or children, she may well succeed in teaching more than children can learn. She naturally loves to tend the sick of her family, and, when she is without family ties, she may, perhaps with advantage, add a knowledge of medicine to her other gifts, and bring comfort to the bedside of strangers. In short, she may exercise her feminine capacities in a more extended field of action than that of her own house; but, should she ever enter fairly into competition with men in all professions, she will have ceased to be woman, though she will not have become man. The experiment, could it really be made on a small scale, would not be without its interest to the students of science, though, from the conditions of the problem, it could never be made to illustrate any theory of the origin of species. To the unwomanly woman it is a virtue to be childless.

A state with an hermaphroditic form of government, if even it could exist for a generation, is by Nature doomed to extinction; it may, however, be worth while to consider what kind of being a woman would become who should take an active part in the election of a representative. As an energetic member of his committee she would have to fight the battle, foot by foot, with his opponents of either sex; she could not always sit at home and restrict herself to the use of a voting paper, because she would then tacitly admit her unfitness for political life with all its hard work and its turmoil of speech making; she would be like a foreigner giving a vote from a distance, without a knowledge of the qualities requisite for success in Parliament. It would be necessary for her to be thoroughly prepared for the fray—breeched instead of petticoated, with a voice hoarse from shouting, with her hair cropped close to her head, with her deltoid muscles developed at the expense of her bust, prepared with syllogisms instead of smiles, and more ready to plant a blow than to shed a tear. She hurries from her husbandless, childless hearth to make a speech on the hustings;

with hard biceps and harder elbows she
forces her way through the election mob; her
powerful intellect fully appreciates all the
ribald jests and obscene gestures of the
British "rough;" she knows the art of
conciliating rude natures, and can exchange
"chaff" with a foul mouthed costermonger;
or, if necessary, she can defend herself, and
blacken the eye of a drunken bargee. She
has learned all the catechism of politics, and
when she mounts the platform she can glibly
recite her duty to the world according to the
side she has chosen. Experience has taught
her the value of invectives, and she
denounces her opponents with a choice
selection of the strongest epithets; at first
she speaks loud in a tone of contentment and
self satisfaction; she ends by losing her
temper and bawling at the top of her voice.
The crowd, never very indulgent, has no
mind to respect a sex which makes no claim
and has forfeited all right to forbearance.
The hardened lines of her face are battered
with apples, brick bats, and rotten eggs—the
recognized weapons of political warfare.
Perhaps the very place where she stands is
the mark of a storming party; and, after
enjoying the glory of an encounter with a
prize fighter (it may be of her own sex), she
is at last brought to the ground by superior
skill and strength. Then probably she retires

to her home; but I, for one, had rather not follow her thither, or into that House of Parliament of which she is destined one day to become an ornament.

Such a description, I am aware, could only be applied to an electioneering woman in modern Britain, and not to an inhabitant of Utopia. In that, or some other republic of the future, not only is woman to be different, but man also; the sexes are to lose their characteristic distinctions not simply by the conversion of woman into man, but by the partial conversion of man into woman. As soon as this sexual compromise has been effected, by means not clearly described, the world will enjoy what enthusiastic heathens used to call the golden age, and what modern enthusiasts of another school now call the millennium. Envy, hatred, malice, and all uncharitableness, will disappear, there will be neither wars nor rumors of wars, and an angelic population will know its own place and limit itself to its own number. Mankind will then have developed itself into a species of gigantic trade union, in which women and their accomplices will infallibly be "rattened" if they create too much competition among men.

A state of society in which humanity shall no longer be human, in which not only sex, but intellect and emotion, shall have been remodelled, and the aspect of the outer world changed by a new and metaphysical cosmogony, is, like the doctrine of abstract right, beyond the grasp of the humble Anthropologist. His occupation will be gone as soon as that era shall commence. But, until then, until murder, theft, and villany of every kind, shall have been extinguished, until that struggle for existence, which pervades all Nature and constitutes the only healthy check upon population, shall have been abolished, until every evil passion shall have been rooted out, he may perhaps be permitted to raise his feeble protest against innovations which would not only subvert man's civilized customs but contradict Nature's first lessons. If statesmanship can amend the laws which press hard upon some unfortunate and exceptional women, if ingenuity can devise harmless occupations for mothers whom prosperity or adversity has deprived of their maternal cares, in short, if any grievance can be met with a remedy which is not opposed to the teachings of science, every human being will have cause for gratitude. If men have met with women who prefer political to domestic life, and despise all conceptions but those which are purely mental, let them in the name of liberty cultivate their acquaintances; but let them also, in the name of liberty and in the name of Nature, permit other men and other women to choose for themselves. If they have but little liking for women who are womanly, if they care nothing for the conversation and the tone of thought which are most in accordance with woman's voice, and mouth, and brain, if they are unable to realize that pleasure which either sex may derive from the sense of intellectual difference, let them by all means endeavor to gratify themselves, according to their own constitution, but let them not, Vandal like, attempt to destroy those beauties which they do not appreciate.—*Anthropological Review*

1.

Book v., cc. iii. to vi.; see, also, the "Laws," book vi., c. xxiii.

www.ingramcontent.com/pod-product-compliance
Lightning Source LLC
Chambersburg PA
CBHW051827250726
48659CB00005B/1717